The Ultimate Quesadilla

Cookbook

All Types of Quesadilla Recipes You Can Try at Home!

By: Owen Davis

Copyright Notice!

Table of Contents

Introduction

We often don't have adequate time to dedicate to our kitchens and bring forth incredible meals. After eating out during lunch, some people will opt to eat out as well during dinner. One thing about eating out is that you might never enjoy freshly cooked and spiced meals to your preference. As a person who looks forward to healthy living, you can dedicate part of your time to creating freshly cooked and delicious meals at home. So, have you been searching for that one cookbook that has plenty of recipes to help you through cooking? Well, look no further. This quesadilla cookbook is packed with sixty nutritious and tasty quesadillas you can prepare on any occasion. Your duty is to simply pick a recipe, gather the ingredients, and follow the simplified directions.

Despite your busy life, these quesadillas will save you a big deal and make you have satisfying meals within minutes. Most of these recipes require you to use a skillet or an oven to give the quesadillas a crispy texture and aromatic flavor.

Your family and friends will always wonder what your secret is when you present to them these incredible quesadillas.

Basics About Quesadillas

Quesadilla's origin is Mexico. If you travel to central and Northern Mexico, be sure to find a wide range of quesadillas. However, you can make these incredible delicacies at your home. You only need to know the basics of preparing the best quesadillas, as explained below.

After preparation of your ingredients, you heat a tortilla using either a pan or oven. It's topped with fillings and cheese; when the cheese melts and the fillings are warm, you take it out of the pan and enjoy!

Now, that said, you'll find lots of variations in this book. Some are double-tortilla quesadillas, requiring flipping. Others require you to fold the tortilla before cooking. Just remember that at the end, you want a crisp, golden-brown quesadilla, heated through and with melted cheese.

Some things to ponder as your plan your next quesadilla cooking include:

Have a pan or skillet large enough to let the tortilla lie flat.

Use flour tortillas. Most supermarkets now have them, especially 9-10" ones. They make hearty quesadillas and are easy to cut—or fold.

When using an oven or a stove, remember to control the heat settings appropriately to get a perfect product.

Don't use too much butter or oil for your quesadillas. This will help you avoid greasy and oily quesadillas.

You can use different ingredients to create an amazing quesadilla.

If you can, prepare your quesadilla filling in advance for the next day.

When planning your ingredients, note the flavors. They should balance well and the cheese too.

Remember that quesadillas cook faster. Don't leave them in the pan for too long; otherwise, they will burn.

Finally, remember to serve your quesadillas while still warm. You won't want that taste of hardened and cold cheese.

1. Squash, Mushrooms, and Peppers Quesadillas

A taste of peppers, mushrooms, squash, and other spices enclosed in a quesadilla is all you need after a tiresome day. Besides, this recipe will nourish your body with adequate vitamins and minerals from the veggies.

Serving Size: 6

Cooking Time: 20 Minutes

Ingredients:

- ½ cup diced red bell pepper
- Cooking spray as needed
- ½ cup diced zucchini
- 6 (9 inches) whole wheat tortillas
- ½ cup diced yellow squash
- 1¼ cups shredded reduced-fat sharp cheddar
- ½ cup diced red onion
- ½ cup diced mushrooms
- 1 tbsp olive oil

Instructions:

Cook the following in a pan coated with a nonstick spray: mushrooms, red pepper, onions, squash, and zucchini for 8 minutes. Set aside.

Add more spray to the pan and add in 1 tortilla. Layer the following on it: 1/8 C. cheese, 3/4 C. veggie mix, 1/4 C. cheese, and another tortilla. Repeat.

Toast the quesadilla for 4 mins per side. Then dice it into two pieces before serving.

2. Avocado-Cauliflower Quesadillas

Cook your quesadilla recipe with a mix of cauliflower and avocado to get good fats, minerals, and vitamins for effective growth. Here is the recipe to try out.

Serving Size: 1

Cooking Time: 10 Minutes

Ingredients:

- 2 tbsps. olive oil
- 2 cups sliced cauliflower florets
- 4 tbsps. Hot sauce
- ½ tsp. Chili powder
- ½ tsp. Garlic powder
- ½ tsp. snipped chives
- 10 inches spinach tortillas
- 3 tbsps. cream cheese
- ½ cup shredded mozzarella cheese
- 1 tbsp. butter
- 1 mashed avocado
- 10 crushed tortilla chips

Instructions:

In a bowl, add the cauliflower, 3 tbsp of the hot sauce, garlic powder, and chili powder, and mix well.

Have a skillet with oil on fire until the oil is hot.

Add the cauliflower mixture and cook for about 3 minutes, mixing often.

Transfer the cauliflower into a bowl.

Add the chives and remaining 1 tbsp of the hot sauce and gently toss to coat.

Place the cream cheese onto the tortilla in a thin layer.

Place the cauliflower mixture onto half of the tortilla, followed by the mozzarella.

Fold the tortilla in half over the filling.

In a nonstick skillet, add the butter and cook until melted.

Place the quesadilla and cook until golden brown from both sides.

Cut the quesadilla into 3 wedges and enjoy with a topping of the avocado, crushed tortilla chips, and chives.

3. Chipotle Quesadillas

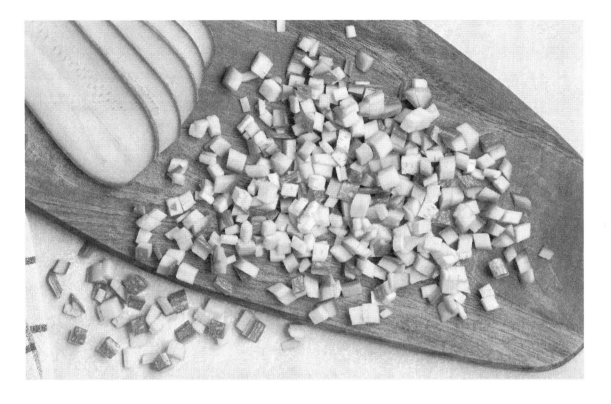

Filled with zucchini, salsa, broccoli, jalapeno, and bell peppers, this satisfying quesadilla recipe is all you need when you have friends coming over. Be sure to include mild spices for an extra kick.

Serving Size: 4

Cooking Time: 20 Minutes

Ingredients:

- 1 chopped zucchini
- 2 tbsp salsa
- 1 chopped broccoli head
- 1 tbsp olive oil
- 1 chopped red pepper
- 8 flour tortillas
- 1 chopped green pepper
- 1 cup grated chipotle cheddar cheese
- 1 chopped onion
- 1 cup chopped jalapeño
- 2 minced garlic cloves
- 1 chopped tomato

Instructions:

In a skillet, add 1 tbsp of the olive oil and cook until heated through.

Add the vegetables except for the tomato and cook for about 5-6 minutes.

Add the tomato and cook for about 2 minutes.

Add the salsa and cook until heated completely.

Place the vegetable mixture onto one side of all the tortillas evenly, followed by the cheese and jalapeños.

Fold each tortilla over the filling.

Heat a skillet and cook the quesadillas until golden brown from both sides, then serve.

4. Hot Dog Quesadillas

This recipe gives you a chance to fix a quick quesadilla using a hot dog when you are hungry but with less time in the kitchen.

Serving Size: 1

Cooking Time: 5 Minutes

Ingredients:

- ¼ cup shredded Cheddar cheese
- 1 turkey hot dog
- ¼ cup bacon & condensed bean soup
- 1 (8 inches) flour tortilla

Instructions:

In a microwave-safe bowl, place the soup.

With a damp cloth, wrap the hot dog & tortilla, place in the soup, and microwave on High for about 30 seconds.

Have hot dog and soup in the center of the tortilla and top with the cheese, then roll.

Microwave for 10 seconds more.

5. Extra Virgin Goat Quesadillas

The nice flavors of goat cheese combined with asparagus and cilantro will melt in your mouth, leaving you wanting more and more. This quesadilla is perfect for kids too.

Serving Size: 4

Cooking Time: 15 Minutes

Ingredients:

- 2 tbsp. extra virgin olive oil, divided
- ½ lb. chopped asparagus
- Salt as desired
- Black pepper to taste
- 2 (10 inches) flour tortillas
- 4 oz. herbed goat cheese
- ¼ cup chopped cilantro
- Fresh cilantro sprigs as needed for garnish

Instructions:

In a skillet, heat 1 tbsp of the olive oil on medium-low heat and cook the asparagus, pepper, and salt till golden browned, stirring occasionally.

Have the goat cheese spread over one side of each tortilla evenly.

Place 1/2 the asparagus and 1/2 the cilantro on each tortilla and fold the tortillas in half to form quesadillas.

Coat the outsides of the quesadillas with the remaining oil.

Place the quesadillas in a skillet on medium-low heat and cook for about 3 minutes from both sides.

Halve the quesadillas and serve with a garnishing of the cilantro.

6. Buffalo Chicken Quesadilla

This quesadilla recipe is a perfect meal plan for outdoor cooking with friends. You can as well opt to serve it for late dinner with your partner.

Serving Size: 2

Cooking Time: 25 Minutes

Ingredients:

- 2 cups shredded rotisserie chicken
- 1/2 cup ranch dressing, divided
- 4 oz. softened cream cheese
- 2 tbsps. sliced green onions
- 1/4 cup + 2 tbsps. buffalo sauce (divided)
- 1/2 cup shredded Monterey Jack
- 1/2 cup shredded Gouda
- Freshly ground black pepper as desired
- Kosher salt to taste
- Vegetable oil as needed for frying
- 4 medium flour corn tortillas

Instructions:

Combine in a medium bowl the chicken, ¼ cup buffalo sauce, cream cheese, green onions, and ¼ cup ranch dressing, stirring until incorporated, along with some pepper and salt.

Heat oil in a large skillet on moderate heat, making sure the bottom is fully coated.

While heating the oil, spread the chicken mixture on top of the tortilla and place it on top of the cheeses, and cover with another tortilla. Do this procedure for the next quesadilla pair.

Cook the quesadilla in hot oil for three minutes until golden brown.

Have a large plate on top of the skillet, invert the skillet and slide the quesadilla onto a platter, and then slide back to the skillet. Cook the quesadilla until golden brown.

Do the second pair of quesadillas with the same steps.

Sprinkle the quesadillas with buffalo sauce and ranch dressing. Spread scallions on top.

7. Hampshire Salmon Quesadillas

Salmon is incredible seafood filled with essential nutrients perfect for our body's functioning. Be sure to serve your whole family this quesadilla for healthy living.

Serving Size: 4

Cooking Time: 10 Minutes

Ingredients:

- 1 peeled and chopped cucumber
- ¼ cup drained and chopped pickled jalapeño pepper
- ½ cup. salsa
- 8 oz. sliced salmon fillets
- 3 tbsps. olive oil, divided
- 2 (4 inches) warmed flour tortillas
- 6 oz. crumbled goat cheese

Instructions:

Put your barbecue grill for medium-high heat and lightly, grease the grill grate.

In a bowl, add the salsa and cucumber and mix well.

Coat the salmon with 2 tbsp of the oil evenly.

Place the salmon onto the grill and cook, covered for about 10-12 minutes, flipping once half way through.

Remove from the grill and place the salmon onto a plate.

With a fork, flake the salmon. Again, set your barbecue grill for medium-high heat and lightly, grease the grill grate.

Place the salmon onto half of each tortilla, leaving 1-inch edges, followed by the cheese and jalapeño pepper.

Enclose the tortillas in half over the filling.

Coat the tortillas with the remaining 1 tbsp of the oil.

Cook the quesadillas onto the grill until golden brown from both sides.

Enjoy alongside the cucumber salsa.

8. Monterey Beef Quesadillas

Monterey Jack cheese has flavors from sweet peppers, rosemary, habanero chilies, garlic, and spicy jalapenos. It is a perfect cheese to make quesadillas because of its authentic taste and aroma.

Serving Size: 4

Cooking Time: 30 Minutes

Ingredients:

- 1½ lbs. beef strips
- 2 tbsps. creole seasoning
- 1 tsp. onion powder
- 1 tsp. Garlic powder
- ½ tsp. black pepper
- 8 oz. shredded Monterey Jack pepper cheese
- 4 tbsps. crumbled feta cheese
- 4 flour tortillas
- Nonstick cooking spray as needed
- 8 oz. sour cream

Instructions:

Have a pan on the fire and cook the beef, creole seasoning, garlic powder, onion powder, and black pepper for about 9-10 minutes.

Drain the grease from the pan.

Place the pepper Jack cheese onto one-half of all tortillas evenly, followed by the feta and beef mixture.

Fold the tortillas gently in half over the filling.

Have a greased nonstick skillet over medium-high heat and cook the quesadillas for about 4-6 minutes, flinging once halfway through.

Halve each quesadilla and enjoy alongside the sour cream.

9. Bacon and Apple Quesadillas

Apples are fantastic fruits that you can consume raw or through recipes. Apart from apple cakes, the apple quesadillas will satisfy your apple craving. Here is an ideal recipe to start with.

Serving Size: 4

Cooking Time: 15 Minutes

Ingredients:

- 4 flour tortillas
- 2/3 cup smoked and shredded Gouda cheese
- 3 cooked and chopped bacon slices
- 1 sliced Granny Smith apple

Instructions:

Set a skillet over medium to high heat.

Add a flour tortilla into the skillet. Add 6 apple slices. Sprinkle 1½ slices of the chopped bacon over the tortilla followed by 1/3 cup of the shredded smoked Gouda cheese.

Place a second tortilla over the top.

Cook until golden and crispy for about 4 minutes per side.

Put onto a plate and repeat with the remaining tortillas.

Slice into wedges and serve immediately.

10. Chicken Fajita Quesadillas with Cilantro Pesto

Once you try these crunchy chicken fajita quesadillas flavored with taco seasoning and serve with cilantro, your family will always ask for more.

Serving Size: 4

Cooking Time: 30 Minutes

Ingredients:

- 1 tbsp. taco seasoning
- ¾ lb. boneless & skinless chicken breasts
- 1/2 cup + 1 tbsp. extra-virgin olive oil, divided
- 1 sliced red onion
- Kosher salt as desired
- 2 cup fresh cilantro leaves and stems
- 2 sliced bell peppers
- 1/4 cup crumbled cotija
- 1 cup fresh basil leaves
- 1 tbsp. butter
- 1 garlic clove
- 1/4 cup almonds
- 8 medium flour tortillas

Instructions:

Cut chicken breast into chunks or strips and coat with 1 tbsp. of oil, salt and taco seasoning.

Cook the chicken in a skillet on moderate heat, turning frequently until thoroughly cooked; place chicken onto a plate.

Have the same skillet, cook the peppers and onions for eight to ten minutes until tender; sprinkle with salt.

Meanwhile, prepare the pesto by pulsing together in a food processor the basil, ½ cup of oil and cilantro until incorporated.

Stir in almonds, garlic, salt, and crumbled cotija; blend until incorporated.

Clean the skillet and melt the butter. Spread the pesto on top of tortilla, place chicken, and top with peppers, onions, and pepper jack.

Cover with another tortilla and cook for three to four minutes, flipping once, until both sides are golden-crisp.

Repeat with the rest of the tortillas, pesto chicken, peppers, onions, and pepper jack.

Serve quesadillas with cilantro pesto and store extra pesto in the fridge for up to 1 week.

11. Sweet Pork Quesadillas

You will love these quesadillas filled with a sweet taste and hearty flavors that will stimulate your taste buds.

Serving Size: 6

Cooking Time: 10 Minutes

Ingredients:

For the sweet pork:

- 1 (3 lbs.) pork shoulder
- 10 oz. el paso sauce
- 1 cup root beer
- 2 cups light brown sugar

For the quesadillas:

- 6 tortillas
- 1 tbsp. butter
- Mexican cheese as needed

Instructions:

Have the pork shoulder into a slow cooker.

In a bowl, add in the el paso sauce, root beer and light brown sugar. Stir well to mix. Pour over the pork.

Cook, covered on the lowest setting for 6 hours. Remove the pork and shred finely. Add back into the slow cooker. Cover and continue to cook on the lowest setting for 2 hours.

Prepare the quesadillas. In a skillet set over medium heat, add the tortillas.

Cook until warmed for a few seconds. Transfer onto a plate.

Spread the butter over the tortillas. Transfer onto quesadilla with the butter side facing down into the skillet.

Spread the shredded pork and shredded Mexican cheese over the top. Top off with another tortillas, with the butter side facing up.

Cook until the cheese is melted for about 3 minutes.

Transfer the quesadilla onto a plate and repeat with the remaining quesadillas.

Serve immediately.

12. Zucchini Button Quesadillas

Zucchini is an incredible vegetable used to prepare salads, cakes, soups, and even quesadillas! Be sure to prepare this quesadilla and enjoy the well-blended flavors.

Serving Size: 2

Cooking Time: 30 Minutes

Ingredients:

- 1 cubed zucchini
- ½ cup shredded sharp Cheddar cheese
- 1 chopped broccoli head
- ½ cup shredded Monterey Jack cheese
- 1 chopped carrot
- 1 chopped yellow onion
- 4 chopped button mushrooms
- 1 chopped red bell pepper
- 4 (10 inches) flour tortillas

Instructions:

Set the broiler of your oven to preheat and line a baking tray using a foil.

In a steamer, place the mushrooms, zucchini, carrot, bell pepper, onion and broccoli set above 1 inch of the boiling water.

Cook, covered for about 2-6 minutes.

Drain well.

Place 2 tortillas onto the ready baking tray in a single layer.

Have the cheddar, veggies, Monterey jack cheese over each tortilla and top each with another tortilla.

Cook in the broiler till golden brown.

Carefully flip the side and cook golden brown.

13. Spicy Crab Quesadillas

These crab quesadillas will stimulate your taste buds, especially if you enjoy seafood. Easy to prep, delicious, and nutritious too.

Serving Size: 1

Cooking Time: 15 Minutes

Ingredients:

- 1/3 cup melted, unsalted butter
- 1 tbsp. chopped cilantro
- ¼ cup vegetable oil
- 1 tsp salt
- ½ cup chopped onion
- 16 (8 inches) flour tortillas
- 2 seeded and chopped jalapeño peppers
- ½ cup shredded jalapeño jack cheese
- 1 minced garlic clove
- 1 lb. drained crab meat
- ¼ cup mayonnaise

Instructions:

Put your oven setting to 375 degrees F before doing anything else

Have a bowl, add the oil and butter and mix well.

In a skillet, add 2 tbsp of the reserved oil mixture over medium heat and cook until heated through.

Cook as you stir the peppers, onion and garlic for about 5 minutes.

Remove from the heat.

Add the crab meat, mayonnaise, cilantro and salt and gently, stir to combine. Coat 1 side of all tortillas with the remaining butter mixture evenly.

In the bottom of baking sheets, arrange the tortillas, buttered side down.

Place the crab meat mixture onto half of each tortilla, followed by the cheese.

Fold each tortilla in half.

Cook in the ready oven for about 4 minutes.

Cut each quesadilla into three portions and enjoy warm.

14. Tangy Tuna Black Bean Quesadillas

This quick quesadilla is filled with black beans, tuna, and cheese, then served with sour cream for maximum satisfaction. Be sure to use whole wheat tortillas for maximum satisfaction.

Serving Size: 4

Cooking Time: 20 Minutes

Ingredients:

- 2 tbsps. hot buffalo wing sauce
- 12 oz. drained tuna
- ½ cup canned, drained sweet corn
- 1 tbsp. garlic salt
- ½ cup shredded Mexican cheese blend, divided
- ½ cup refried black beans
- 1 tsp. ground cumin
- ½ cup low-fat sour cream
- 1 tbsp. butter, divided
- 4 (9 inches) tortillas whole-wheat tortillas

Instructions:

In a bowl, combine black beans, tuna, and sour cream. Mix them together. Add the corn, garlic salt, buffalo sauce, cumin, and garlic salt. Mix them all in.

Have ½ tbsp. butter in a pan large enough to take a quesadilla. Put a tortilla in the pan for a few seconds and flip. Put half of the tuna mix on it and spread over the whole tortilla. Scatter half of the cheese over the tuna, and top with another tortilla.

Cook, covered for one minute.

Turn the quesadilla and over the pan again. Cook until the cheese melts—it should take another 1-2 minutes.

Repeat the process for the other quesadilla.

Slice each into eight pieces and serve.

15. Smoky Mushroom Quesadillas

The tangy taste, the amazing texture, and the aroma that comes with these smoky mushroom quesadillas will leave you yearning for more. Be sure to be extra creative in the kitchen while making these quesadillas and enjoy.

Serving Size: 4

Cooking Time: 30 Minutes

Ingredients:

- 1 tbsp tomato paste
- 4 (8- to 10-inches) whole-wheat tortillas
- 1 tbsp. cider vinegar
- ¾ cup shredded Monterey Jack cheese
- 1 diced onion
- 2 tsps. canola oil
- 1 minced chipotle chile in adobo sauce
- 1 tbsp. canola oil
- 1 lb. diced portobello mushroom caps
- ½ cup prepared barbecue sauce

Instructions:

Have a bowl, mix together the chipotle, barbecue sauce, vinegar and tomato paste.

In a large nonstick skillet, heat 1 tbsp of the oil on medium heat and cook the mushrooms for about 5 minutes, stirring occasionally.

Add the onion to cook for about 5-7 minutes.

Combine the mushroom mixture into the bowl of the barbecue sauce until even.

Place the tortillas onto a smooth surface and spread 3 tbsp of the cheese on ½ of every tortilla and about 1/2 C. of the mushroom mixture.

Halve and enclose the tortillas in half.

Have a skillet, heat 1 tsp of the oil on medium heat and cook 2 quesadillas for about 3-4 minutes, turning once.

Keep warm on a cutting board enclosed in a foil as you finish with other quesadillas.

Serve cut in wedges.

16. Bean Quesadillas

When making this bean quesadilla, pack it with plenty of varied veggies for an authentic taste and flavor. Also, the veggies add extra nutritional value required in our bodies.

Serving Size: 12

Cooking Time: 20 Minutes

Ingredients:

- 1 tbsp. vegetable oil
- 1 chopped onion
- 1 cup shredded cheddar cheese
- 2 minced garlic cloves
- 15 oz. drained black beans
- 1 chopped green bell pepper
- ¼ cup vegetable oil
- 2 chopped tomatoes
- 10 oz. frozen corn
- 12 (12 inches) flour tortillas

Instructions:

Have a skillet set over medium heat, add in 1 tbsp of vegetable oil. Add in the onion and minced garlic—Cook for 5 minutes or until soft.

Add in the drained black beans, chopped green bell pepper, chopped tomatoes, and frozen corn. Stir well to mix.

Cook until hot, about 3 minutes.

On 6 of the flour tortillas, spread the bean and vegetable mix over the top. Sprinkle the shredded cheddar cheese over the filling. Top off with the remaining tortillas.

Have a separate skillet set over medium to high heat, add in ¼ cup of vegetable oil. Add in the quesadillas.

Cook until crispy on both sides, for 4 minutes.

Transfer onto a plate. Slice into wedges and serve immediately.

17. BBQ Chicken & Pineapple Quesadillas

This satisfying recipe is perfect for a person who enjoys sweet and spicy meals. Are you that person? Well, here is your perfect quesadilla recipe.

Serving Size: 5

Cooking Time: 30 Minutes

Ingredients:

- 2 boneless & skinless chicken breasts
- 1/2 diced yellow onion
- 1 1/4 cups sweet and spicy BBQ sauce, divided
- 1/2 sliced pineapple
- 1 cup shredded cheddar cheese
- 5 medium whole wheat flour tortillas
- Cilantro as needed for serving

Instructions:

Preheat the oven at 350 degrees F.

Have a baking sheet by lining the bottom with foil and spray with nonstick spray.

Place the chicken on top of foil and spread with one-half cup BBQ sauce with a spoon to evenly coat the chicken.

Garnish onions over the chicken.

Bake for twenty minutes until thoroughly cooked. Remove chicken from oven and shred using two forks.

Combine in a bowl the shredded chicken, onions, and ½ cup of BBQ sauce until well coated.

Spread the chicken mixture on the half part of the tortilla and then garnish with pineapple and top with cheese.

Place a tablespoon of BBQ sauce on the other half of the tortilla.

Close the tortilla by gathering the side with BBQ sauce to the opposite side.

Do the remaining tortillas and ingredients with the same procedure.

Spray a grill pan with nonstick spray and heat on medium heat.

Have the quesadillas, one at a time in the pan and cook for two to three minutes, then cook the other side for one to two minutes until the whole quesadilla is browned.

Cook the remaining quesadillas in batches. Slice and garnish with cilantro and serve.

18. Mediterranean Quesadillas

This cool quesadilla is filled with Mediterranean-approved foods, including cheese, tomatoes, olives, and zucchini. You don't have the be on a specific diet to enjoy this healthy meal.

Serving Size: 4

Cooking Time: 25 Minutes

Ingredients:

- 1 tsp. olive oil
- 1/2 cup shredded mozzarella cheese, divided
- Cooking spray as needed
- 1/3 cup chopped onion
- 1/2 cup diced tomato, divided
- 1/4 cup crumbled feta cheese, divided
- 1/2 tsp. minced garlic
- 1/4 cup of chopped pitted kalamata olive, divided
- 4 (8 inches) fat-free flour tortillas
- 1/8 tsp. salt
- 1 1/4 cups shredded zucchini
- 1/4 tsp. dried oregano
- 1/8 tsp black pepper

Instructions:

In a nonstick skillet, add the oil over medium-high heat until heated through.

Add the garlic and onion and stir fry for about 2 minutes.

Add the zucchini and stir fry for about 3 minutes.

Remove from the fire, then stir in the oregano, salt and pepper.

Place mozzarella onto 2 tortillas evenly, followed by the zucchini mixture, tomato, olives and feta.

Cover with remaining tortillas.

Grease another skillet with the cooking spray and place over medium heat until heated through.

Place 1 quesadilla and cook for about 2 1/2 minutes per side.

Repeat with the remaining quesadilla.

Cut each quesadilla in half and enjoy warm.

19. Instant Rice Quesadillas

Instant rice is a perfect ingredient, especially when you just arrived at home and are feeling extremely hungry. You can fix a meal quickly and enjoy it. Wondering how? Well, here is an incredible quesadilla recipe for you.

Serving Size: 8

Cooking Time: 25 Minutes

Ingredients:

- 6 chicken breast tenders
- 2 (0.36 oz.) packets sazon seasoning
- 1 cup water
- 2 tbsps. butter
- 1 cup instant rice
- 14 oz. rinsed and drained black beans
- 1 tsp. garlic salt
- 1 tsp garlic salt
- 16 oz. shredded Mexican cheese blend
- 8 extra-large flour tortillas
- 1 tbsp. softened butter

Instructions:

In a pan, melt 2 tbsp of the butter on medium heat and cook the chicken, and 1 tsp garlic salt, and 1 pack sazon seasoning for about 8-10 minutes, shredding chicken.

Have a pan, add water and rice and bring to a boil.

Reduce the heat to low and simmer, covered for about 5-10 minutes.

In a microwave-safe, mix together 1 teaspoon of garlic salt, black beans, and 1 packet sazon seasoning, and microwave for 3 minutes.

Stir the black bean mixture to the rice until even.

Have the tortillas onto a smooth surface.

Place the bean-rice mixture over ½ of each tortilla, then Mexican cheese, then shredded chicken, and more of Mexican cheese.

Fold the tortillas in ½, then spread some softened butter on top.

Have a skillet, large enough on fire over medium heat and cook each quesadilla with the butter-side down for about 10 minutes, turning halfway.

Serve in wedges.

20. Hot Pear Quesadillas

When pears are plenty in season, get into the kitchen, get creative and explore different meal ideas as you nourish your body with this incredible fruit. Here is among the best quesadilla recipe you can make with the pears.

Serving Size: 10

Cooking Time: 20 Minutes

Ingredients:

- 12 oz. chilled and stripped Brie cheese
- 2 ripe and sliced pears
- 2 tbsps. olive oil
- 1/2 sliced red onion
- 2 sliced jalapeño peppers
- 6 inches flour tortillas

Instructions:

Place the Brie cheese onto the bottom half of each tortilla evenly, followed by the pear and jalapeño slices.

Have the tortillas fold in half over the filling.

In a skillet, add 1 tsp of the oil and cook until heated through.

Have 1 quesadilla cook until golden brown from all sides.

Repeat with the remaining quesadillas and enjoy.

21. Turkey Quesadillas

When having some left-over turkey meat, it is the right time to consider making this recipe. You only add a few more flavorful ingredients to make a nutritious and satisfying quesadilla.

Serving Size: 6

Cooking Time: 5 Minutes

Ingredients:

- 1/4 lb. shredded cooked turkey meat
- 2 tbsps. cranberry sauce
- 1/2 minced jalapeno pepper
- 1 sliced green onion
- 2 flour tortillas
- 2 tbsps. chopped cilantro
- 1/2 cup shredded Cheddar cheese

Instructions:

Have a skillet with one tortilla, large enough on the fire.

Add with 1/2 of the Cheddar cheese, then turkey, then cranberry sauce, followed by jalapeño pepper, then green onion and finally the remaining Cheddar cheese.

Have the remaining tortilla over the top.

Cook until done, about 4 minutes per side.

22. Sloppy Joe Quesadillas

Instead of the usual bun bread, stuff your meat and cheese ingredients on tortillas to create satisfying quesadillas. This recipe is perfect for serving your guests because of its spicy and saucy taste.

Serving Size: 4

Cooking Time: 30 Minutes

Ingredients:

- 1/2 chopped onion
- 1 tbsp. extra-virgin olive oil
- 1 lb. ground beef
- 2 garlic cloves
- 1/3 cup brown sugar
- 1/2 cup ketchup
- 1 tbsp. chili powder
- 1 cup shredded Monterey Jack
- 2 tbsps. mustard
- Black pepper as desired
- Kosher salt to taste
- 1 cup shredded cheddar
- 4 medium flour tortillas

Instructions:

Have the olive oil in a large skillet on medium heat and sauté the onions for five minutes until tender.

Stir in the garlic to cook for thirty seconds until aromatic.

Add the beef and cook for six to eight minutes until pink color has vanished. Remove excess fat.

Stir in brown sugar, ketchup, chili powder, salt and pepper; simmer for five minutes until thickened.

Place mixture onto a plate and wipe out the skillet. Place the flour tortilla in the skillet over moderate high heat.

Place on top of tortilla the beef mixture, cheddar cheese and Monterey Jack; cover with the second tortilla.

Cook for two minutes each side, flip once, until both tortillas are golden brown and the cheese is melty.

Repeat the procedure for the remaining tortillas and ingredients.

Slice quesadillas into wedges. Serve warm.

23. Corned Beef and Cabbage Quesadilla

Do you want a tasty treat to serve during your next celebration party? Then this is the perfect quesadilla dish for you to prepare.

Serving Size: 4

Cooking Time: 25 Minutes

Ingredients:

- 4 flour tortillas
- 10 slices of Swiss cheese
- 24 thin slices of corned beef
- ½ cup drained sauerkraut
- Thousand island dressing as needed for dipping

Instructions:

Set a skillet over medium heat.

Have one side of a flour tortilla brushed with butter. Place into the skillet with the butter side facing down.

Add a slice of Swiss cheese, 6 slices of corned beef, 2 tbsps. of sauerkraut and another slice of Swiss cheese. Top off with a second tortilla.

Cook until done for about 4 minutes on each side. Transfer onto a plate.

Repeat with the remaining flour tortillas.

Slice into wedges and serve with the Thousand Island dressing for dipping.

24. Seafood Quesadillas

Give your seafood a twist from the usual stews and baked seafood recipes by preparing this satisfying quesadilla. Use any seafood you have or enjoy the most.

Serving Size: 6

Cooking Time: 60 Minutes

Ingredients:

- 3 tbsps. vegetable oil
- 1 sliced onion
- 1 sliced red bell pepper
- 1 sliced green bell pepper
- 1 tsp. salt
- 1 tsp. ground cumin
- 1 tsp. chili powder
- 1 lb. peeled and deveined shrimp
- 1 minced jalapeno pepper, seeded
- 1 juiced lime
- 6 large flour tortillas
- 3 cups shredded Mexican cheese blend, divided

Instructions:

Have a large skillet, heat 2 tbsp of the vegetable oil on medium-high heat, and sauté the green bell pepper, onion, and red bell pepper for about 6-8 minutes.

Stir in the salt, cumin, and chili powder.

Stir in the shrimp and cook for about 3-5 minutes.

Remove the skillet from the heat and stir in the jalapeño pepper and lime juice.

Have a skillet, heat 1 tsp of the oil on medium heat.

Place a tortilla in hot oil.

Place about 1/6 shrimp filling and a half cup of Mexican cheese blend on one side of the tortilla.

Fold the tortilla in half.

Cook for about 5 minutes

Carefully flip the side and cook for about 3-5 minutes.

Repeat with remaining tortillas and filling.

25. Chicken, Bacon and Mushrooms Quesadillas

Can you imagine mushrooms, bacon, and chicken all in a quesadilla? The taste is incredible, the flavors just perfect, the texture and the look simply appetizing.

Serving Size: 5

Cooking Time: 30 Minutes

Ingredients:

- 1 lb. sliced chicken breast meat
- 1/2 tsp salt
- 2 cups shredded mozzarella cheese
- 1/2 tsp. black pepper
- 2 tbsps. olive oil
- 14 precooked and diced turkey bacon slices
- 8 oz. sliced fresh mushrooms
- 1 cup Alfredo sauce
- 1 tsp butter
- 5 large flour tortillas

Instructions:

Stir fry your chicken for 12 mins in oil after seasoning it with pepper and salt.

Set aside, remove excess oils from the pan, and julienne your chicken.

For 6 mins, cook your mushrooms and bacon in the same pan. Then set the heat to low. Add in your Alfredo sauce and chicken. Cook for 3 mins.

Get another pan and toast your tortillas in melted butter.

Add 1/5 of your chicken mushroom mix on one side of the tortilla. Then put 1/5 of your cheese. Fold the other side to form a quesadilla. Cook for 4 mins per side.

Repeat for all ingredients. Once everything is done. Cut each quesadilla in half and serve.

26. Steak Quesadillas

The exact taste of these quesadillas will make you love quesadillas even more. The steak, avocado slices, and the cheese mixture blends just perfect for a cool meal experience.

Serving Size: 4

Cooking Time: 30 Minutes

Ingredients:

- 1½ lbs. flank steak, pat-dried and sprinkled with pepper and salt
- Ground black pepper to taste
- Kosher salt as desired
- 2 cups shredded Monterey Jack
- 2 cups shredded cheddar
- 1 lime
- 2 avocados
- 2 cups of Pico de Gallo
- 8 pieces flour tortillas

Instructions:

Preheat the grill and oven at 375° degrees Fahrenheit.

Combine in a small bowl the Monterey Jack and cheddar cheeses, set aside.

Cut the avocados into half, remove the pits and flesh from skin with a large spoon. Cut one avocado into one-fourth-inch slices and squeeze out juice from lime; cover in plastic. Set aside.

Chop the rest of the avocado and mix together with Pico de Gallo, set aside.

Place steak in the preheated grill, cook for five to six minutes per side for medium doneness.

Place grilled steak on a plate; cover loosely with foil, let stand for five minutes before cutting into diagonal thin slices.

Line two rimmed sheet pans with a parchment paper and place the tortillas.

Spread one-half cup of cheese mixture, and layer with avocado slices and steak. Add another layer of ½ cup cheese and cover with tortilla.

Do the rest of the quesadillas and bake for ten minutes until the cheese has melted.

Serve with Pico de Gallo and avocado salsa after slicing into wedges.

27. Cherry Chicken Quesadillas

Cherry tomatoes have a soft texture and are small in size. Yes, they make incredible salad recipes. However, when you cook them in quesadillas, they bring out the best taste.

Serving Size: 4

Cooking Time: 16 Minutes

Ingredients:

- 4 flour tortillas
- 2 cups shredded Cheddar cheese
- 2 cups cooked shredded chicken
- 1 cup fresh spinach
- ½ cup chopped cherry tomatoes
- 1 tbsp. vegetable oil

Instructions:

Have your oven set to 350 degrees F before doing anything else.

Arrange the tortillas on a baking sheet and spread 1/2 C. of the Cheddar cheese over each.

Leave in the oven to cook for about 5 minutes.

Remove from the oven.

Have a large skillet on medium heat and cook the chicken, spinach, and tomatoes for about 5 minutes.

Place the chicken mixture over each tortilla evenly and fold in half.

Grease the same skillet with a thin layer of oil and heat on medium heat.

Cook the tortillas in batches for about 3 minutes per side.

28. Korean Beef Quesadillas

Experience the taste of Korean cuisine with these beef quesadillas. The beef mixture spread on each tortilla is a blend of garlic, brown sugar, soy sauce, and red pepper flakes, ginger and sesame seeds, which adds a touch of Korean to your Mexican dish.

Serving Size: 4

Cooking Time: 30 Minutes

Ingredients:

- 1½ lbs. ground beef
- 1/3 cup soy sauce
- 1/4 cup brown sugar
- 1 tbsp. sesame seeds
- 3 crushed cloves of garlic
- 1/4 tsp. crushed red pepper flakes
- 1 tbsp. grated fresh ginger
- 6 chopped scallions
- 3 cups shredded mozzarella
- 8 large flour tortillas

Instructions:

Have a large skillet coated with cooking spray and place the beef; stir often until browned.

Prep the sauce by combining in a small bowl the brown sugar, garlic, soy sauce, sesame seeds, red pepper flakes and ginger, whisking to combine well.

Pour the sauce into the browned beef, cook and stir for five minutes, set aside.

Have the same skillet coated with cooking spray and heat up again.

Place one tortilla in the skillet and spread on top with ¾ cup of beef mixture, and coat the top with ¾ cup mozzarella, and cover the cheese with 2 tbsps. scallions.

Cover the top with another tortilla, pressing down using a dinner plate.

Cook until the bottom tortilla is browned, flip over to the opposite side; cook for an additional three minutes until both sides are browned.

Place cooked tortilla on a cutting board and do the rest of the 3 quesadillas following the instructions above and serve.

29. Steak Fajita Quesadillas

There come those evenings when you don't know what to prepare for dinner. Well, this steak quesadilla will save you the worry of thinking about what to prepare.

Serving Size: 4

Cooking Time: 15 Minutes

Ingredients:

- 2 tbsps. vegetable oil, divided
- 1/2 sliced onion
- 1/2 sliced green bell pepper
- Salt to taste
- 4 flour tortillas
- ½ lb. cooked and sliced steak
- 1 cup shredded Mexican cheese blend

Instructions:

Using a skillet, the tortillas will fit in (10-inch is perfect), heat 2 tsp of oil; medium heat is perfect. Cook the onion and green pepper for 5-10 minutes, enough to soften the onion. Salt to taste and place in a bowl.

Take the rest of the oil and brush each tortilla on one side.

Place the oiled side of a tortilla in the skillet using medium heat. Put half of the steak, onion/pepper mix, and the shredded cheese on the tortilla. Top with another tortilla oiled-side up, and press down.

Cook on each side until browned and the cheese melted for about 4 minutes.

Remove and repeat in the same skillet.

Cut each quesadilla into wedges and serve.

30. Old Bay Shrimp Quesadillas

Old bay seasoning is among the best seafood seasoning used to spice up meals, mostly fish and seafood. It is a combination of varied spices such as black pepper, salt, paprika, celery salt, and red pepper flakes.

Serving Size: 4

Cooking Time: 20 Minutes

Ingredients:

- 4 large flour tortillas
- 2 cup chopped spinach
- 3 cups shredded Monterey Jack, divided
- 1 tsp. Old Bay seasoning
- 2 tbsps. butter
- 1 cup guacamole
- 1½ lbs. medium shrimp
- 1/4 cup chopped cilantro
- 1 chopped tomato
- Dash of cayenne pepper

Instructions:

Rinse, devein and remove tails of shrimp, set aside.

Preheat the oven to 400° Fahrenheit.

Line two rimmed sheet pans with a sheet of parchment paper. Put two tortillas on each pan.

Combine in a medium-sized bowl two cups of Monterey Jack cheese and spinach, set aside.

Have the butter in a large pan on moderate-high heat to melt.

When the butter becomes bubbly, add the Old Bay seasoning and toss the shrimp until coated.

Cook, stirring until the shrimp is no longer pinkish. Spread an even layer of the cheese-spinach mixture on the half portion of each tortilla.

Evenly layer the shrimp on top of the mixture and place it on top with the remaining cheese mixture.

Fold the tortilla over and sprinkle on top of the quesadilla with the remainder of the cheese.

Bake for ten minutes until melted.

Garnish with guacamole, chopped tomato, chopped cilantro, and a dash of cayenne pepper. Serve hot.

31. Strawberry Cheesecake Quesadillas

This is a creamy and fruity quesadilla dish that you can prepare whenever you are craving something on the sweet side.

Serving Size: 2

Cooking Time: 10 Minutes

Ingredients:

- 4 (8 inches) flour tortilla
- 2 tbsps. soft cream cheese
- 2 tbsp. strawberry jam
- 1 tbsp. powdered sugar

Instructions:

Spread ½ of the cream cheese onto one side of 2 of the tortillas.

Spread the strawberry jam over the tortillas. Top off with the remaining tortillas

Have a skillet set over medium heat, add in the quesadillas. Cook for 5 minutes on each side or until golden. Transfer onto a plate.

Serve dusted with powdered sugar.

32. Spinach and Mushroom Quesadillas

The creaminess of cheese combines with the earthiness of the mushrooms and freshness of the spinach to make a satisfying snack or light meal. Sour cream and guacamole are perfect accompaniments.

Serving Size: 4

Cooking Time: 20 Minutes

Ingredients:

- 1 (10 ounces) package chopped spinach
- 2 cups shredded cheddar cheese
- 2 tbsps. butter
- 2 sliced garlic cloves
- 2 sliced Portobello mushroom caps
- 4 (10 inches) flour tortillas
- 1 tbsp. vegetable oil

Instructions:

Have the oven set to preheat to 350 degrees F (175 degrees C).

Following the directions on the package, prepare the spinach. Drain. Pat the spinach dry.

On one half of a tortilla, scatter ½ cup of cheese. Do this for all the tortillas.

Place the tortillas on a baking sheet—cheese side up. Bake for five minutes; the cheese should be melted. Remove from oven.

In a pan, melt butter using medium heat. Add the mushroom and garlic, stir, and cook for five minutes.

Add the spinach to the pan, stir, and cook for another five minutes.

Divide the spinach/mushroom mix into quarters, and put one quarter on each tortilla, on top of the cheese. Fold each over on top of the filling.

In another pan, heat the oil using medium heat. Put a quesadilla in the pan. Cook three minutes per side; the quesadilla should be golden brown. Repeat for the three remaining quesadillas.

Quarter each and serve.

33. Parmesan Pepper Quesadillas

Bell peppers combined with cheese to make a quesadilla is the ideal meal option for a quick lunch when having the ingredients in the kitchen.

Serving Size: 4

Cooking Time: 10 Minutes

Ingredients:

- 1 tbsp. chopped green pepper
- 4 medium tortillas
- 1/4 cup Parmesan cheese
- 2 tbsps. oil
- 1/2 cup grated cheddar cheese
- 1/4 cup chopped green onion
- 1 1/2 tbsps. mayonnaise

Instructions:

Set your barbecue grill for medium heat and lightly, grease the grill grate.

In a bowl, add the Parmesan cheese, cheddar cheese, mayonnaise, green pepper and green onion and mix until well combined.

Place the cheese mixture onto 2 tortillas evenly.

Cover with the remaining 2 tortillas.

Coat the both sides of each quesadilla with the oil evenly.

Cook your quesadillas onto the grill for about 5 minutes and serve.

34. Spinach and Artichoke Quesadillas

If you love the taste of classic spinach and artichoke dip, then this is the perfect quesadilla dish for you. One bite and I know you will become hooked.

Serving Size: 4

Cooking Time: 10 Minutes

Ingredients:

- ¼ tbsp. extra virgin olive oil
- 1 cup shredded mozzarella cheese
- 8 oz. drained and chopped artichoke hearts
- 6 oz. baby spinach leaves
- 4 oz. cream cheese
- ¼ cup of shredded parmesan cheese
- 8 flour tortillas

Instructions:

Have a skillet set over medium to high heat, and then add in the flour tortillas.

Cook until warm for a few.

Have a pot set over medium to high heat, and add the olive oil. Add in the chopped artichoke hearts. Cook for 1 minute. Lower the heat to low. Add the spinach leaves.

Cook until wilted for about 2 minutes. Add in the cream cheese, shredded mozzarella cheese and shredded parmesan cheese.

Stir in some salt and black pepper. Cook for 5 minutes or until melted. Remove from heat.

Spread ¼ cup of the mix onto 4 of the tortillas. Top off with the remaining tortillas.

Have a separate skillet set over medium heat, add in 1 teaspoon of olive oil. Add the tortillas.

Cook until crispy for about 4 minutes. Transfer onto a plate and repeat.

Slice into wedges and serve.

35. Philly Cheese Steak Quesadilla

In this recipe, you need to load the tortilla shells with peppers & onions, pepper jack cheese, roast beef, cheddar, and Swiss cheese before roasting the quesadilla to perfection. The taste is amazing, and you will enjoy the wide range of ingredients.

Serving Size: 2

Cooking Time: 30 Minutes

Ingredients:

- ⅛ sliced onion
- ¼ cup grated pepper jack cheese
- ¼ sliced pepper
- 4 sliced deli roast beef lunch
- 2 tbsps. butter (divided)
- ¼ cup grated cheddar cheese
- ¼ cup grated Swiss cheese
- 2 flour tortillas

Instructions:

Melt in skillet 1 tbsp. butter on moderate high heat.

Sauté the peppers and onions until tender crisp. Set aside from the fire.

Melt the rest of the butter in another pan on medium heat and add the tortilla shell.

Sprinkle on top of tortilla the cheddar cheese and layer on top with roast beef.

Sprinkle on top of beef the shredded jack cheese, and place on top of pepper jack cheese the peppers and onions.

Sprinkle on top of veggies the Swiss cheese layer and cover with another tortilla shell.

Cook the quesadillas until the bottom of tortilla shell turns golden brown, flipping once until the other tortilla turns golden brown.

Remove from pan and portion into quarters when slightly cooled. Serve!

36. Caramel Apple Cheesecake Quesadilla

This quick-to-fix quesadilla filled with apples is a perfect meal idea for a simple but healthy breakfast. You can as well opt to serve it for snacking.

Serving Size: 1

Cooking Time: 15 Minutes

Ingredients:

- 1 sliced Granny Smith apple
- 2 tsps. sugar
- 1/3 cup softened cream cheese
- 2 pieces 8" flour tortillas
- Butter as needed for greasing
- Caramel sauce as desired for drizzling

Instructions:

Preheat a large nonstick pan on moderate heat.

Mix together in a small bowl the cream cheese and 1 tsp. Sugar. Set aside.

Brush exterior of tortillas with a pat of butter. Slather the inside of another tortilla with a cream cheese mixture.

Place tortilla in a skillet with cream cheese side facing up and arrange on top the sliced apples. Place the other tortilla with the butter side facing up.

Cook for three minutes until crisp golden, flip once, and cook for two minutes longer until golden and the cream cheese mixture is thoroughly warmed.

Remove tortilla from heat and sprinkle on top with 1 tsp. Sugar.

Drizzle with caramel sauce. Cut into wedges and serve.

37. BLT Quesadillas

These crispy and delicious quesadillas are packed full of crispy bacon and a spicy cheese blend that you will want to make every night of the week.

Serving Size: 2

Cooking Time: 20 Minutes

Ingredients:

- 6 crispy bacon strips
- 8 oz. grated pepper jack cheese
- 4 (10 inches) flour tortillas
- 1 chopped tomato
- 1 cup chopped Romaine lettuce
- ¼ cup sour cream
- 1 juiced lime
- Dash of salt and black pepper

Instructions:

In a bowl, add in the lettuce, some salt, chopped tomato, and black pepper.

Have a separate bowl, add in the sour cream and lime juice. Stir well until evenly blended.

In a skillet set over low to medium heat, add in the bacon. Cook for 5 minutes or until crispy, then slide onto a plate lined with paper towels. Crumble. Drain the excess grease.

Clean the skillet and set over medium heat. Add in 1 tortilla. Top off with the grated pepper jack cheese and crumbled bacon.

Top off with the second tortilla.

Cook until crispy, for about 4 minutes. Repeat with the remaining tortillas. Transfer onto a plate.

Serve with the salad and sour cream.

38. Chicken with Pico De Gallo Quesadillas

For an easy meal, try these flour tortillas wrapped around the classic combination of chicken, onions, peppers, and cheese. The key for this meal is the pico de gallo as it brings everything together, and raises these quesadillas to the level of superb!

Serving Size: 2

Cooking Time: 30 Minutes

Ingredients:

- 2 diced tomatoes
- 2 tbsps. olive oil, divided
- 1 chopped onion
- Black pepper to taste
- 1 sliced green bell pepper
- 2 juiced limes
- 2 tbsps. chopped cilantro
- 1 minced jalapeño pepper
- Salt as desired
- 1 cup shredded Monterey Jack cheese
- 2 stripped boneless & skinless chicken breast halves
- 2 minced garlic cloves
- 4 (12 inches) flour tortillas
- 1/2 sliced onion
- 1/4 cup sour cream, for topping

Instructions:

Mix the diced tomatoes, chopped onion, minced jalapeno, cilantro, and lime juice together in a bowl. Reserve.

Have one of the tablespoons of olive oil in a sizable skillet to heat. Sauté the chicken thoroughly; make sure the juice runs clear. Remove and reserve.

Heat the rest of the olive oil. Sauté the green pepper & onion; make sure the smell is good and strong. Add half the pico de gallo and chicken, and thoroughly mix. Place the skillet aside and keep the mix warm.

In another pan, heat one of the tortillas. Spread ¼ cup of the cheese over the tortilla. Top with half the chicken mix.

Sprinkle ¼ cup of the cheese on top of the chicken, cover with a second tortilla. Cook until the bottom is light golden-brown. Flip and cook the other side—the cheese should have started melting. When the other tortilla has lightly browned, remove from the skillet.

Repeat the process with the remaining ingredients.

Serve topped sour cream and the remaining pico de gallo after slicing into wedges.

39. Sweet Potato and Bean Quesadillas

This is a delicious quesadilla dish that even the pickiest of eaters won't be able to turn down once they try a bite for themselves. It is perfect to make for those with food sensitivities.

Serving Size: 4

Cooking Time: 60 Minutes

Ingredients:

- 2 peeled and sliced sweet potatoes
- 2 tbsps. extra virgin olive oil
- 2 tsps. powdered cumin
- ½ tsp. of sea salt
- 2 tbsps. vegan butter spread
- 4 gluten free tortillas
- Refried beans as needed
- Havarti cheese slices as desired for topping
- 1 sliced avocado for topping

Instructions:

Preheat the oven to 425 degrees.

In a greased baking dish, add in the sweet potato slices, extra virgin olive oil, powdered cumin and dash of sea salt.

Stir well to mix, then have it into the oven to roast for 40 minutes or until soft. Remove and set aside to cool.

Have a skillet set over medium heat, add in ½ tbsp. of the vegan butter spread. Add a tortilla into the skillet.

Have a layer of refried beans spread over the tortilla. Add a layer of the sweet potatoes followed by 2 slices of Havarti cheese.

Have the tortilla fold over the filling and press slightly.

Cook until crispy on both sides, about 4 minutes per side, then slide onto a plate as you finish up the other quesadillas.

Serve immediately after slicing into wedges with the avocado slices.

40. Southwestern Corned Beef Quesadillas

If you have been to New Mexico, you have heard a taste of this incredible quesadilla. Wondering how you can make them at home? Well, use this recipe for perfection.

Serving Size: 2

Cooking Time: 15 Minutes

Ingredients:

- 1/2 cup leftover shredded corned beef brisket
- 2 (8 inches) flour tortillas
- 1/2 cup shredded Monterey Jack cheese
- 2 tbsps. diced green chilies

Instructions:

In the microwave, heat the brisket for 30 – 60 seconds; the setting should be high.

Over medium heat, heat a pan. Put in a tortilla. Spread the cheese, brisket, and chilies over the tortilla—cheese first. Put the other on top.

Cook until the bottom tortilla has browned nicely—it should be golden; it will take around 2-4 minutes. Flip and repeat for the other side—cook for another 2-4 minutes.

Cut the quesadilla in half (or more slices) to serve.

41. Cheesy Crab and Shrimp Quesadillas

When hanging out with your friends, this creamy and buttery quesadilla packed with cheese, crab meat, and green onions makes a perfect meal choice for the time. Besides, it is loaded with ingredients that will leave you satiated for hours.

Serving Size: 16

Cooking Time: 30 Minutes

Ingredients:

- 2 oz. diced celery
- 2 oz. butter
- ¼ tsp. thyme
- 2 oz. diced onion
- 10 oz. heavy cream
- 10 oz. white wine
- 2 tbsps. lemon juice
- 1 tsp. Old Bay seasoning
- 1/2 lb. cooked bay shrimp
- 1/2 lb. crab meat
- 6 oz. bread crumbs
- 1/2 lb. cream cheese
- 2 oz. Parmesan cheese shredded
- 1 lb. & 2 oz. shredded cheddar cheese
- 8 (12 inches) tortillas

For serving:

- 1 lb. Pico de Gallo
- 1 lb. sour cream

Instructions:

Have the butter in a saucepan and melt on medium heat.

Sauté the onions, thyme and celery until the onions are transparent and the butter has melted.

Pour heavy cream and white wine into the mixture, bring to a boil and simmer on low heat.

Season mixture with Old Bay seasoning, stir in lemon juice and cream cheese until thoroughly mixed.

Remove saucepan from heat and add crab meat, shrimp, bread crumbs, Parmesan and cheddar cheese; stir until incorporated.

Have the saucepan back to the heat and stir the mixture on low heat until the cheeses have melted. Set aside.

Meanwhile, preheat a large pan on moderate heat and lightly coat the entire bottom of pan.

Place tortilla in hot pan and top with two ounces of cheddar cheese.

When the bottom of tortilla turns brown and the cheese is melty, add the six ounces of crab dip on the half part of the tortilla, spreading wide to cover half of the tortilla; folding over the cheese about half of the tortilla onto the homemade crab dip.

Lightly press and remove from pan.

Cut quesadilla into wedges. Serve with sour cream & Pico de Gallo.

42. Beef Pepperoni Pizza Quesadilla

Whenever in the kitchen, you don't limit your capabilities when preparing quesadillas. For instance, this recipe may appear of Italian touch, but it is a real quesadilla you can make and enjoy with your family and friends.

Serving Size: 4

Cooking Time: 10 Minutes

Ingredients:

- 2 medium flour tortillas
- 1 tbsp. extra-virgin olive oil
- 2 minced cloves garlic
- 1/3 cup pizza sauce
- ½ cup grated Parmesan
- 1 cup shredded mozzarella
- ¼ tsp. Italian seasoning
- 1/3 cup sliced beef pepperoni
- Freshly chopped parsley as needed for garnishing.

Instructions:

Preheat broiler and heat oil in a large heat-proof skillet on medium heat.

Place one tortilla into the skillet, spread half of the pizza sauce.

Spread garlic on top of pizza sauce and sprinkle on top of garlic with half of each: mozzarella cheese, Parmesan cheese, beef pepperoni, and Italian seasoning. Cover with another tortilla.

Cook Pizzadilla until golden-crisp and the cheese melts.

Flip Pizzadilla by covering the skillet with a large plate; invert the skillet to transfer Pizzadilla onto a large plate. Slide the Pizzadilla back to the skillet with the cooked side facing up.

Sprinkle on top with the last batch of pizza sauce, mozzarella cheese, Parmesan cheese, beef pepperoni, and Italian seasoning.

Put the skillet on top of the broiler and cook for two minutes until the beef pepperoni is crisp-tender and the cheese melt.

Sprinkle parsley on top, then serve.

43. Simple Jam Quesadillas

Are you craving something sweet? Well, prepare this satisfying quesadilla any time during the day and enjoy the sweetness. Use any jam preserve you enjoy the most.

Serving Size: 2

Cooking Time: 5 Minutes

Ingredients:

- 1 tbsp butter
- 4 (6 inches) tortillas
- 6 tbsp jam, any flavor

Instructions:

Place half of the jam onto 2 tortilla shells evenly, leaving about 1/2-inch from the edges.

Cover with the remaining tortillas.

In a skillet, add half of the butter over medium heat and cook until melted.

Place 1 quesadilla and cook until golden brown from both sides.

Repeat with the remaining quesadilla.

Cut each quesadilla into quarters and enjoy warm.

44. Cheese Salsa Quesadilla

If you have never tried outdoor quesadillas, this is a perfect recipe to start with. Fill your tortillas and grill on a foil for nice flavors.

Serving Size: 1

Cooking Time: 10 Minutes

Ingredients:

- ¼ chopped red onion
- 1 diced tomato
- ½ lime
- A small handful of chopped cilantros
- 1/2 cup shredded Tex-Mex cheese
- 1 large tortilla

Instructions:

Combine in a medium-sized bowl the tomato, juice of ½ lime, cilantro, and onion, set aside.

Divide foil into two pieces about 12" by18" and put on top of another.

Place the tortilla on top of the foil, and spread half of the tortilla with Tex-Mex cheese.

Fold tortilla, folding up packet to seal tightly.

Place packet on hot grill and cook for five minutes, flip at least once. Remove the packet from the grill, let it cool slightly.

Unfold and top with tomato salsa, then serve.

45. Chicken Gorgonzola Quesadillas

Are you a Gorgonzola fan? Well, add some spinach, chicken, and other flavorful ingredients to prepare this satisfying quesadilla and serve with sour cream.

Serving Size: 2

Cooking Time: 30 Minutes

Ingredients:

- 2 chopped and pounded skinless, boneless chicken breast halves
- Salt as desired
- Black pepper to taste
- 1 tbsps. olive oil
- 1/2 chopped onion
- 2 minced garlic cloves
- 2 flour tortillas
- 5 oz. crumbled Gorgonzola cheese
- 1 cup cooked spinach

Instructions:

Put the oven settings to preheat at 350 degrees F (175 degrees C). Grease a baking sheet.

Have a pan with oil over medium heat. Put the chicken, salt, and pepper in. Stir and cook until the chicken is not pink and the juices are clear.

Put in the onion and garlic. Stir. Cook, occasionally stirring for 10-15 minutes; the onion should be golden-brown.

On the baking sheet, put a tortilla. Spread ½ of the Gorgonzola on it. Then, add the chicken and spinach, spreading them over the tortilla. Top with the rest of the Gorgonzola cheese. Have the other tortilla on top and press down.

Bake the quesadilla for around 10 minutes; the cheese should be melted. Cut into six or eight wedges.

46. Caramelized Onion and Steak Quesadillas

This is a dish you can make whenever you have leftover steak. It is simple to prepare and perfect after a long day at the office.

Serving Size: 1

Cooking Time: 12 Minutes

Ingredients:

- 1 oz. sliced leftover steak
- 2 slices of Havarti cheese
- Dried thyme to taste
- ¼ sliced onion
- 2 tbsps. barbecue sauce
- Butter as needed
- 2 tbsps. garden vegetable cream cheese

Instructions:

Have a skillet set over medium to high heat, add in 1 tbsp. of butter. Add in the sliced onions. Cook for 5 minutes or until soft.

Add in the sliced steak. Cook for about 2 minutes or until hot.

Add in the barbecue sauce and continue to cook for an additional minute.

Spread the cream cheese over the tortilla. Add 1 slice of Havarti cheese over the top. Transfer into a separate skillet.

Top off with the steak mix. Add another slice of Havarti cheese over the top. Fold the tortilla over the filling.

Cook about 4 minutes or until crispy on both sides.

Remove and slice into wedges. Serve immediately.

47. Picnic Quesadillas

Like the name, this tasty quesadilla filled with grilled sirloin steak and cheese is a perfect accompaniment during a picnic experience with a loved one.

Serving Size: 4

Cooking Time: 15 Minutes

Ingredients:

- 4 flour tortillas
- 3/4 cup shredded cheddar cheese
- 8 oz. grilled and sliced sirloin steaks
- 1 minced jalapeño
- 3/4 cup salsa, drained of excess liquid
- 1 tbsp. vegetable oil

Instructions:

Have about 1/4 C. of the cheese onto each of 2 tortillas evenly, followed by the steak, jalapeño, 1/4 C. of the salsa and remaining cheese.

Cover with the remaining tortillas and press to seal.

In a skillet add 1 1/2 tsp of the oil over medium heat and cook until heated through.

Have the quesadillas, 1 at a time cook for about 4-6 minutes, flipping once half way through.

Enjoy warm.

48. Yellow Squash and Chicken Quesadillas

Did you know the difference between summer and winter squash? Well, the difference is that summer squash is picked when immature. Besides, they take only 50 days to mature, and they spoil quite faster. On the other hand, winter squash takes 100 days to mature, and they can be stored for months without going bad.

Serving Size: 2

Cooking Time: 15 Minutes

Ingredients:

- ½ cubed red bell pepper
- 2 minced garlic cloves
- 1 tbsp. chopped fresh cilantro
- Salt as needed
- 1 tbsp. olive oil
- ½ cubed yellow squash
- ¾ cup diced rotisserie chicken meat
- 4 whole-wheat tortillas
- Sharp Cheddar cheese as needed
- Olive oil cooking spray
- ½ mashed avocado
- ½ cup rinsed and drained canned black beans

Instructions:

Have a skillet, heat 1 tbsp of the olive oil on the fire and sauté the garlic until fragrant.

Add yellow squash and sauté for about 1-2 minutes.

Stir in the bell pepper, salt and chicken, then stir fry for about 3 minutes, then put into a bowl.

Have one tortilla sprayed with olive oil cooking spray, then place it the ready skillet.

Add one slice of the Cheddar cheese, then 1/2 of the chicken mixture, then 1/2 of the black beans, and 1/2 of the avocado, and finally ½ of the cilantro.

Have another tortilla sprayed with cooking spray, then place on top of the filling.

Cook for about 8 minutes, filliping once, then keep warm as you finish cooking the other quesadillas.

49. Breakfast Quesadillas

Give your breakfast experience an extra kick by preparing this sweet and flavorful quesadilla filled with sweet apples and other sweet ingredients.

Serving Size: 2

Cooking Time: 10 Minutes

Ingredients:

- 1 diced Honeycrisp apple
- 2 tbsps. light corn syrup
- 1 tbsp. honey
- 1 tbsp. maple syrup
- ½ tsp. ground cinnamon
- 1 tsp. brown sugar
- 2 (11 inches) flour tortillas

Instructions:

Have a large skillet over medium-low heat, then cook the apple, maple syrup, corn syrup, brown sugar, honey, and ground cinnamon for about 8-10 minutes, stirring every few minutes.

Transfer the apple mixture into a bowl.

Have 1 tortilla in the same skillet over medium-low heat and top with the apple mixture evenly.

Have the remaining tortilla on top and cook for about 1-3 minutes per side.

50. Sausage and Chilies Quesadillas

Poblano chilies combined with sausages bring out a mild and tangy taste that will have you hoping for more. Perfect for sharing with friends.

Serving Size: 4

Cooking Time: 20 Minutes

Ingredients:

- 1 tbsp canola oil
- 1 tbsp canola oil
- 2 minced smoked beef sausage links
- 1/4 cup sour cream
- 1/4 cup salsa
- 1 minced Poblano chili
- 1/2 minced red bell pepper
- 1/2 minced red onion
- 1/2 cup frozen corn kernels
- 4 flour tortillas
- 2 cups shredded Colby cheese

Instructions:

Cook the following in 1 tbsp of canola for 16 mins: corn, sausage, red onions, Poblano and red peppers.

Layer a fourth of the sausage mix on one side of your tortillas. Then fold the other side to make a quesadilla. Do this for all the tortillas.

Get a 2nd pan and cook each quesadilla in 1 tbsp of canola for 4 mins per side until the cheese is bubbly.

Once all the quesadillas have been cooked cut them in half.

Enjoy with a dollop of salsa and sour cream.

51. Spinach Quesadillas

Cooking spinach in muffins and cakes isn't the only way to have your kids enjoy this nutritious vegetable. Cook them in quesadillas using this recipe and enjoy them with your family.

Serving Size: 4

Cooking Time: 20 Minutes

Ingredients:

Relish:

- ½ sliced red onion
- ¾ cup oil-cured black olive
- 2 tbsps. grated lemon zest
- 2 tbsps. red vinegar
- ¼ cup extra virgin olive oil
- Salt as needed
- Black pepper, to taste

Quesadillas:

- 12 (6 inches) flour tortillas
- 2 cups grated white cheddar cheese
- 1 cup crumbled feta
- 6 oz. Baby Spinach
- Salt to taste
- Black pepper as needed
- 1 tbsp. olive oil

Instructions:

For the relish: in a bowl, add all the ingredients and mix until well combined.

Place in the fridge with the bowl covered before using.

Have your grill set for medium heat and lightly grease the grill grate.

Place the cheeses onto eight tortillas evenly, followed by the spinach, and sprinkle with the salt and pepper.

Arrange four filled tortillas onto the other two filled tortillas, filling side up.

Cover with the remaining plain tortillas.

Coat the top of each quesadilla with the oil evenly.

Arrange the quesadillas onto the grill, oiled side down, and cook for about 2 minutes.

Carefully flip each quesadilla and cook, covered for about 1-2 minutes.

Cut each quesadilla into quarters and enjoy with a topping of the relish.

52. Heirloom Quesadillas

You only need a collection of several vegetables and cheddar cheese to improve the flavor of this heirloom quesadilla. You will get maximum minerals and vitamins out of these quesadillas.

Serving Size: 6

Cooking Time: 15 Minutes

Ingredients:

- 1 chopped red bell pepper
- 1 tbsp olive oil
- ½ cup chopped zucchini
- Cooking spray as needed
- ½ cup chopped yellow squash
- 6 (9 inches) whole wheat tortillas
- 1 chopped red onion
- 1¼ cups shredded sharp Cheddar cheese
- ½ cup chopped mushrooms

Instructions:

Have a nonstick pan, large enough with oil over medium, then cook the red pepper, onion, yellow squash, mushrooms, and zucchini for about 7 minutes.

Transfer the vegetables into a large bowl.

Have the pan you had used greased with the cooking spray.

Have a tortilla in the pan and sprinkle with about 1/4 C. of the cheese evenly.

Top with ¾ cup of the mushroom mixture and sprinkle with more 1/8 C. of the cheese.

Finish with another tortilla and cook for about 4 minutes on each side.

Have the quesadilla from the pan.

Repeat with the remaining ingredients.

Portion each quesadilla into eight triangles and serve hot.

53. Shrimp and Mango Quesadillas

Ripe mangos blend perfect in seafood, especially when paired with shrimp. This could be your ideal quesadilla when craving a meal with mild flavors and nutritious.

Serving Size: 4

Cooking Time: 20 Minutes

Ingredients:

- 2 tbsps. vegetable oil
- ½ lb. peeled shrimp, tails removed
- ¼ tsp. salt
- 1/8 tsp. black pepper
- 6 oz. soft cream cheese
- 1 cup shredded cheddar cheese
- ¼ cup chopped cilantro
- 4 tbsps. soft butter
- 1 peeled and chopped mango
- 4 flour tortillas

Instructions:

Have a skillet set over medium to high heat, add in the shrimp, salt and black pepper to cook for about 5 minutes or until bright pink. Transfer into a bowl and set aside.

In a bowl, add in the cream cheese, shredded cheddar cheese and chopped cilantro. Stir well to mix. Add with a dash of salt and black pepper.

Chop the shrimp into small pieces.

Place a skillet over medium heat. Add 1 tbsp. of butter onto one side of the tortillas. Place into the skillet with the butter side facing down. Spread the cream cheese mix over half of the tortilla.

Top off with ¼ cup of the chopped shrimp and ¼ cup of mango. Gently fold over the clear half of the tortilla over the filling. Cook for 2 to 3 minutes or until soft.

Keep warm onto a plate and repeat with the remaining tortillas.

Slice into wedges. Garnish with the chopped cilantro and remaining mango.

Serve immediately.

54. Poblano Pepper (Grilled) and Mango Quesadillas

You can use a variety of peppers for this quesadilla; the peppers you use will make this either mild or spicy, but you'll have the lovely fruitiness of peppers and mango.

Serving Size: 2

Cooking Time: 30 Minutes

Ingredients:

- ¼ cup melted butter
- 8 oz. softened cream cheese
- 1 diced mango, peeled
- 16 (10 inches) flour tortillas
- 1 minced poblano pepper

Instructions:

Put the grill on medium heat to preheat.

Have half of the tortillas spread with 2 tbsps. cream cheese, then mango and poblano peppers, and have another tortilla on top, pressing gently.

Coat the butter over the top and bottom quesadillas evenly.

Put them on the grill. Grill them for 5 minutes per side—they should be golden-brown.

Remove them from the grill and serve after slicing into wedges.

55. Blueberry and Brie Quesadillas

This is a crazy good and delicious quesadilla dish I know you are going to want to make as often as possible. It is the perfect treat for breakfast or dessert.

Serving Size: 4

Cooking Time: 10 Minutes

Ingredients:

- 4 (10 inches) flour tortillas
- 1/3 lb. brie cheese, evenly divided
- 1 tbsp. light brown sugar
- ¼ tsp. powdered cinnamon
- 6 oz. blueberries, evenly divided
- 3 tbsps. chopped walnuts, evenly divided
- 1 tbsp. half and half
- ¼ cup powdered sugar

Instructions:

In a bowl, add in the powdered cinnamon and light brown sugar. Stir well to mix. Reserve ¼ teaspoon of this mix and set aside the remainder.

In a separate bowl, add in the powdered sugar, half and half and ¼ teaspoon of the sugar mix. Whisk well to mix and set aside.

Have a skillet over medium heat and grease with cooking spray.

Spread the brie cheese over the quesadillas. Place one of the tortillas into the skillet. Sprinkle the blueberries and walnuts over the top followed by half of the remaining sugar mix. Cover with a second tortilla.

Cook them for 4 minutes on each side or until crispy.

Put onto a plate and repeat with the remaining tortillas.

Serve immediately after cutting into wedges with the glaze.

56. Caribbean Quesadillas

Here's a family-friendly dish perfect for a sizzling summer day. Swiss cheese, pineapple, and bacon combine with chicken to give you a sweet/salt combination which will be requested over and over.

Serving Size: 4

Cooking Time: 25 Minutes

Ingredients:

- 8 (10 inches) flour tortillas
- 2 cups chopped cooked chicken
- 1/4 cup honey mustard
- 1 1/2 cups shredded Swiss cheese
- 2 tbsps. butter
- 1 1/2 cups unsweetened pineapple tidbits, drained
- 2 tbsps. pineapple preserves
- 1/2 cup cooked crumbled bacon

Instructions:

Put the oven settings to 250 degrees F (120 degrees C).

Combine the pineapple preserves and honey mustard in a bowl. Spread ¼ of the mix over each tortilla; keeping about an inch from the edge.

Evenly distribute the cheese, chicken, and crumbled bacon over the spread.

Top each with another tortilla.

Over medium heat, heat up a large pan. Melt ½ tbsp. in the pan. Tilt it to make sure the butter covers the surface.

Put a quesadilla in the pan. Fry until lightly browned; the cheese should be melted. It will take about 1½ minutes on each side.

Put the finished quesadillas in the ready oven while you cook the rest.

Cut each into six wedges. Arrange with pineapple garnish in the center and serve.

57. Wild Rice, Corn, and Black Bean Quesadillas

This recipe is among the top meatless Monday quesadilla—simple, easy, and delicious. Rice, corn, and black beans combine with salsa to make an easy lunch or dinner. You can vary this one by including pickled jalapeños. Avocado, hot sauce, and sour cream also work.

Serving Size: 2

Cooking Time: 30 Minutes

Ingredients:

- 8 oz. Ready Rice Long Grain & Wild
- 1 cup shredded sharp Cheddar cheese
- 1/2 cup reduced-sodium black beans, rinsed and drained
- 1/2 cup frozen sweet corn, thawed
- 2 chopped green onions
- 4 (10 inches) flour tortillas
- 1/2 cup mild salsa

Instructions:

Following the directions on the package, prepare rice

In a bowl, combine rice, corn, shredded cheese, beans, and green onions. Mix thoroughly.

On one half of each tortilla, put a quarter of the mix. Put 2 tbsps. of the salsa on top. Fold the tortillas in half.

Use cooking spray to grease a pan large enough to hold a quesadilla. Heat using medium-high heat.

One quesadilla at a time, place in the pan and cook until lightly golden-brown; it should take about 1-2 minutes on each side.

Repeat, spraying the pan as needed.

Cool them just a bit, and halve them. Serve; provide more of the salsa if you'd like.

58. Pulled Pork and Caramelized Onion Quesadillas

Caramelized onions and pulled pork make these quesadillas an all-time favorite. The hidden secret why they taste so good is to cook the onion in butter and olive oil until caramelized, and then seasoned with sugar, salt and pepper. Never forget to serve quesadillas with BBQ sauce.

Serving Size: 4

Cooking Time: 30 Minutes

Ingredients:

- 1 tsp. olive oil
- 3 tbsps. butter, divided
- ½ tsp. brown sugar
- 1 sliced yellow onion
- 8 small tortillas
- Salt as desired
- Black pepper to taste
- 2 cups shredded Monterey jack cheese
- 2 cups cooked pulled pork

For dipping:

- Barbecue sauce as needed

Instructions:

Melt in a large skillet 1 tbsp. of butter on medium low heat.

Pour the olive oil and cook the onions for thirty minutes until caramelized and golden brown.

Top with a pinch of brown sugar, salt and pepper. Remove skillet from heat, set aside.

Have 4 tortillas on a clean work surface and spread each with equal amount of cheese.

Evenly spread caramelized onions on top of cheese and pulled pork on top of onions; cover with a second tortilla.

Heat ½ tbsp. of butter in a large pan on medium heat until melted.

Cook quesadilla in batches for two to four minutes until the bottom turns golden-brown.

Flip and cook the opposite side for two to four minutes until the cheese has melted.

Do the rest of quesadillas and slice into four quarters. Drizzle with BBQ sauce.

Serve!

59. Oreo Cheesecakeadilla

Surprise your loved ones with these Cheesecakeadilla, which makes use of Oreos and cream cheese as filling. The outside of one tortilla is dabbed with butter and place on top of the other tortilla with the Oreo filling facing up. Crushed Oreos are spread on top of the buttered side when serving.

Serving Size: 4

Cooking Time: 15 Minutes

Ingredients:

- 1/4 cup crushed Oreos
- Additional Oreos for garnish
- 1/3 cup softened cream cheese
- Pat of butter
- 1 tsp. sugar
- 2 (8 inches) flour tortillas

Instructions:

Place on medium heat a large nonstick pan.

Mix together in a small bowl the crushed Oreos and cream cheese.

Coat the exterior part of tortillas with a pat of butter while slathering the interior with Oreo-cream cheese mixture.

Place Cheesecakeadilla in the skillet with cheese side facing up and cover with the other tortilla with butter side facing up.

Cook for three minutes until golden-crisp, flipping once and cook the opposite side for two minutes.

Remove Cheesecakeadilla from heat and sprinkle with sugar.

Sprinkle with crushed Oreos.

Enjoy!

60. Raspberry-Nutella Cheesecakeadilla

This quesadilla is filled with Nutella-cream cheese mixture and the raspberry sauce is spooned over to bathe the Cheesecakeadilla to your sweet tooth's delight. Instead of the usual meat and vegetable filling, this recipe reshapes your thoughts about quesadilla.

Serving Size: 4

Cooking Time: 10 Minutes

Ingredients:

- 2 tbsps. Nutella
- 1 cup raspberries
- 1/3 cup softened cream cheese
- 2 tsps. sugar
- 2 pieces 8-inch flour tortillas
- Pat of butter for greasing

Instructions:

Combine in a saucepan the raspberries with 1 teaspoon of sugar; cook and stir on low heat for five minutes until the berries are broken down and thickened.

Remove saucepan from heat, let raspberries cool. Set aside.

Combine in a small bowl the Nutella and cream cheese, set aside.

Heat a large nonstick pan on moderate heat.

Coat the outsides of tortillas with a pat of butter; slathering the inside with Nutella-cream cheese mixture.

Place tortilla in the pan with cream cheese side up and top with the other tortilla with the butter side up.

Cook Cheesecakeadilla for three minutes until golden-crisp. Flip the other side and cook for two minutes until golden-crisp.

Remove Cheesecakeadilla from heat and sprinkle with the last batch of sugar.

Spoon the raspberry spoon to coat the Cheesecakeadilla all over.

Cut into wedges and serve.

Enjoy!

Conclusion

Thank you for having this incredible cookbook and reading it through the end.

It is my hope that this cookbook has served you your intended purpose. If you have been admiring different quesadilla recipes from different platforms but don't know how to go about the whole cooking process, this book has simplified everything for you.

Probably, you have noticed how easy it is to prepare these quesadillas and how beneficial they are. Above all, I hope you have realized how you can incorporate different ingredients to make incredible quesadillas!

The next action for you to take is to do your grocery shopping, pack your kitchen well, and dedicate your free time to cooking satisfying quesadillas and enjoy with your family.

We wish you a happy cooking journey as you explore quesadilla cooking in your kitchen!

Appendices

Hey, guys! I just wanted to say thanks for supporting me by purchasing one of my e-books. I have to say—when I first started writing cookbooks, I didn't have many expectations for myself because it was never a part of "the plan." It was more of a hobby, something I did for me and decided to put out there if someone might click on my book and buy it because they liked my food. Well, let me just say it's been a while since those days, and it's been a wild journey!

Now, cookbook writing is a huge part of my life, and I'm doing things I love! So, THANK YOU for trusting me with your weekly meal preps, weekend BBQs, 10-minute dinners, and all of your special occasions. If it weren't for you, I wouldn't be able to concentrate on producing all sorts of delicious recipes, which is why I've decided to reach out and ask for your help. What kind of recipes would you like to see more of? Are you interested in special diets, foods made with kitchen appliances, or just easy recipes on a time-crunch? Your input will help me create books you want to read with recipes you'll actually make! Make sure to let me know, and your suggestions could trigger an idea for my next book…

Take care!

Owen

Printed in Great Britain
by Amazon

13943831R00093